Contents

Introduction
Minimizing the risk

Sport is exciting, enjoyable and good for you. We need to exercise in order to keep our bodies healthy, and sport is an excellent way to exercise. Taking part in sport is also an ideal environment for making friends, learning to be part of a team, or just having fun and enjoying yourself. However, we also have to remember that sports injuries are very common. For example, every year in the USA around 2.5 million people between the ages of 5 and 24 attend hospital because of sports injuries. The sport with the highest injury rate associated with young people is basketball.

Basketball
In the USA, basketball injuries affect about 447,000 people under 24 every year. The pattern of injuries shown by US statistics like these is the same throughout the world.

Some sports are more likely to involve injury than others. You are more likely to sustain an injury during snow sports than when taking part in track events, for example. But the vast majority of injuries are avoidable, and just by taking a few sensible precautions, you can make sure that you continue to enjoy your favourite sport rather than missing out on the action with an injury.

SPORTS

Wayland

an imprint of Hodder Children's Books

White-Thomson Publishing Ltd,
2-3 St Andrew's Place, Lewes,
East Sussex BN7 1UP

Published in Great Britain in 2004 by Hodder Wayland, an imprint of Hodder Children's Books

This paperback edition published in 2006

This book was produced for White-Thomson Publishing Ltd by Ruth Nason.

Design: Carole Binding
Picture research: Glass Onion Pictures

British Library Cataloguing in Publication Data
Sarah Lennard-Brown
    Sports Injuries. - (Health Issues)
    1.Sports injuries – Juvenile literature
    I.Title
    617.1'027

ISBN 0 7502 4484 4

Printed by C&C Offset Printing Co.,Ltd.,China

Hodder Children's Books
A division of Hodder Headline Limited
338 Euston Road, London NW1 3BH

Acknowledgements

The author is especially grateful to Anne Hinton-van'tHoff for her help and encouragement in the preparation of this book. The author and publishers thank the following for their permission to reproduce photographs and illustrations: Corbis: pages 4 (Tom Stewart), 6 (Tom Stewart), 35 (Chuck Savage), 39 (LWA-JDC), 49 (Ronnie Kaufman), 55 (DiMaggio/Kalish); Angela Hampton Family Life Picture Library: pages 21, 31, 54; Popperfoto.com: cover and pages 1, 11, 13, 14, 25, 43, 50l, 50r, 58; Science Photo Library: pages 3 and 41 (BSIP Keene); Topham/ImageWorks: pages 8, 37, 46, 53, 56; Topham/PA: pages 33, 42; Topham/Photri: page 9; Topham/ProSport: page 16; Topham/UPPA Ltd UPPA.co.uk: pages 19, 23, 26. The illustrations on pages 12, 17, 28, 34, 44, 46 and 52 are by Carole Binding.

Note: Photographs illustrating the case studies in this book were posed by models.

Every effort has been made to trace copyright holders. However, the publishers apologise for any unintentional omissions and would be pleased in such cases to add an acknowledgement in any future editions.

Learning how to cope with an injury is a vital part of being a good sports player. All professional players have to cope with an injury at some point. Learning to recognize that you have a problem, reporting the injury to your coach or parents and following the medical advice necessary for recovery are all part of being a sportsman or woman.

This book investigates the causes of sports injuries, the effects they have on the sports player, and how the injuries are treated. It also discusses how to prevent injuries. In Chapter 1, we consider the background to sports injuries: the importance of keeping fit and staying healthy; issues concerning young people and how injuries affect them; the facts and myths surrounding women and sports injuries; and the basic principles that govern sporting safety.

The following chapters look at specific parts of the body and the variety of sporting injuries that can affect them. We investigate treatments and first aid for common injuries. Each chapter concludes by focusing on a particular sport where injury to the body area in question may occur. Specific issues to do with injury prevention are considered and there are tips on how to stay safe when playing sport.

Injury in sport is common, but it does not have to spoil your enjoyment. The better informed you are about sports injuries, the less likely you are to suffer from one, and the better able you are to handle an injury if it does occur.

Types of injury

Sports injuries typically fall into one or more of these categories:

- **Cuts and grazes**, *varying in severity from a mild graze, which does not break the skin but can be painful, to a laceration involving heavy bleeding and needing medical treatment.*
- **Bruises**, *sometimes called contusions, which are formed when a blood vessel bleeds into the skin or muscle without any break in the skin.*
- **Muscular strains**, *which occur when a muscle is over-stretched or pushed beyond its ability.*
- **Sprains**, *which involve the over-stretching of a ligament (a thick band of fibres that connect one bone to another).*
- **Fractures** *(breaks or cracks in bone), which can be open (the bone sticks through the skin) or closed.*
- **Dislocation**, *where a joint is displaced from its normal alignment.*

1 Ready for action
Sports health and safety

Sport is good for you. Participating in sporting activities can help your body to become fitter and your brain to be more alert and active. It can also be an excellent way of meeting people with similar interests and making friends.

A fitter body

Taking part in sport can increase your general strength and stamina, tone up your muscles and strengthen your bones. It can help improve your balance, coordination and mobility and increase your body's resistance to disease. It can help keep your heart healthy, and regular weight-bearing exercise can help prevent osteoporosis (a condition where bones become brittle and weak).

The World Health Organization (WHO) estimates that regular moderate physical exercise reduces a person's risk of developing heart disease, diabetes, colon cancer and lower back pain by up to 50%. The WHO also states that regular moderate physical exercise can help control body weight and can prevent or reduce the likelihood of developing high blood pressure. High blood pressure can result in stroke or heart disease.

Feeling fine
Sport can help you to feel better about yourself and others.

A happier mind

Regular moderate exercise can reduce stress, anxiety and feelings of depression. It can help improve the way you feel about yourself and your life. Exercise improves blood flow all over your body and this includes your brain. The brain therefore has a plentiful supply of oxygen and nutrients so that it can perform at its best. So regular moderate exercise can help you to perform better at school and help you to stay alert during lessons.

Taking part in sports can also make you feel happier and more confident, so that it is easier to talk to the people you meet at sports events. And a shared interest in sport gives you something interesting to talk about. This can make it easier to make friends.

Some sports activities have a very active social scene that goes with them. This is particularly true of team sports, where the sense of loyalty and belonging that grows on the sports field leads to lots of social activity off the sports field. Sports such as football, baseball, rugby, cricket and basketball often have a social aspect and may organize nights out, parties and other social events.

There is some evidence that regular moderate exercise can affect the way you behave. People who exercise regularly are less likely to be in trouble with the police or involved in activities that can threaten their wellbeing, such as taking drugs. However, despite all these benefits, the World Health Organization estimates that 60% of the world's population do not exercise enough.

Health benefits

Regular moderate exercise:

- can help control body weight
- can help you to feel happier about yourself
- can help reduce stress and anxiety
- can help you to make friends
- helps build healthy bones and muscles
- helps reduce the risk of developing osteoporosis as you get older
- reduces the risk of developing heart disease
- reduces the risk of developing colon cancer
- reduces the risk of developing diabetes
- reduces the risk of developing high blood pressure.

How much?

Regular moderate exercise involves doing enough activity to make your heart beat faster for at least 20 minutes three times a week.

The likelihood of injury

Participating in sport is good for you, but it should always be treated with respect. All sports carry some risk of injury. The sports that are more likely to result in injury are contact sports (where physical contact occurs between players, such as rugby, judo and American football) and sports that involve hurling yourself over, under or onto things, such as gymnastics, pole vaulting and ski jumping.

You are less likely to be injured if you are healthy. You are more likely to sustain a sporting injury if you are unfit or unwell. You should avoid sporting activity if you have an existing injury or a high body temperature due to illness.

Our bodies need to be looked after to ensure that they are in good condition and strong enough to endure sporting demands. In order to perform at their best, sportsmen and sportswomen need to be aware of several factors, such as how to eat healthily and how to choose suitable sportswear and equipment.

Six sports

In the USA 17% of all sporting injuries to people between the ages of 10 and 19 occur in six sports: baseball, basketball, cycling, American football, skating and soccer.

Healthy diet
Eating a balanced diet including lots of fruit helps keep your body in good working order.

Training to be the best

'My training regime is very tough. I swim nearly every day and work out at the gym to keep my whole body strong. I have to watch what I eat, go to bed early and generally keep myself in good condition. My coach works out my training regime, based on my performance and what condition my body is in. If I am getting tired or I have an injury, then we focus on different things. The better you get at a sport, the more focused and scientific you have to be. The difference between winning and losing can be in hundredths of a second. I want to be the best, so I have to train for it.'
(Mark, aged 15)

Diet

Professional sports players know that, in order to perform well in their sport, they need to look after their body properly. They have to keep their body weight within a healthy level – not too heavy and not too light. Carrying too much body weight makes it harder to move and uses up more energy. Being underweight often means that you may get tired quickly and can reduce your strength and stamina. What is a healthy weight varies from person to person, depending on body type and height. Participating in regular moderate exercise can help to regulate your body weight and keep you healthy.

What you eat is also important. It affects not only your body weight but also how you feel and how your body works. Eating at least five servings of fruit and/or vegetables a day will help ensure that your body gets enough vitamins and minerals. These are needed to help you grow properly and to help your body repair itself and fight infections. Professional sportsmen and sportswomen tend to eat a diet that has a lot of carbohydrates (like wholemeal bread, pasta and rice) and fruit and vegetables, but is quite low in fat.

Strength and stamina

It is vital to 'listen to' your body and treat it with respect. You need to be aware of what you are capable of, and not push your body too far. Injuries are more likely when you are over-tired or have pushed your muscles beyond their capability. When starting a new sport, you should increase the amount of exercise you do gradually. It takes time for your body to grow muscles and for your stamina levels to increase.

*'Running is the thing, man …
on a good day I feel like I'm flying.'
(Eliot, aged 16,
long-distance runner)*

Equipment

Suitable, well-maintained equipment, correctly used, is essential to prevent sports injuries. Many injuries are caused by broken equipment or equipment being misused. An American study in 1999 found that 55% of injuries to young people playing baseball were due to impact between the bat or the ball and a part of the body (usually the head). The same study found that, when injuries to adults playing baseball were included, overall 12% of injuries were equipment-related.

Sportswear is also very important. You should always wear the correct safety equipment for the sport you are participating in. The correct footwear is vital. Taking part in sport in the wrong shoes can put you at far greater risk of injury from falls and trips, as well as foot and leg injuries.

Young people and sports injuries

Young people have to take particular care when participating in sports. Young people vary enormously in size, shape, strength and rate of growth. Bones, tendons, muscles and ligaments are more susceptible to injury when they are growing. Growth spurts cannot be predicted, so extra care is needed to prevent injury.

*'Some days I'm so tired. I've
grown over an inch in the last few
months – it's really affected my game.'
(Alex, aged 14, hockey player)*

The bigger and stronger you are, the more likely you are to suffer injury when you fall over or bang into something.

The bigger you are, the more force is exerted at the collision point. During puberty, a sudden increase in hormones racing around your body, combined with spurts of muscle and bone growth, can cause you to become more clumsy than usual. Clumsiness together with increased body size and weight makes sports injuries more likely.

Individuals

During adolescence people grow at different rates.

Deaths due to sporting injuries are very rare, but children under the age of 10 have a higher risk of sporting fatality. The smaller size of young children's chest and abdomen and softer bones mean that they are more likely to sustain severe internal injuries from hard impacts. In the USA, 3 or 4 children die every year from being hit in the chest or head by a baseball. In other parts of the world, children are similarly at risk from being hit by hard balls in games such as cricket or golf. Wearing proper safety equipment and using a softer ball can prevent many of these injuries.

Under 15s

In the USA, more than 3.5 million sports-related injuries to people under the age of 15 are reported every year.

Growth plate injuries

Growth plates are areas at the end of the long bones in your body, where bone is still growing and being formed. Your long bones are in your upper and lower arms, upper and lower legs, fingers and toes. The growth plates stop functioning and turn into strong bone when you have finished growing (at about age 20 for boys and often several years earlier for girls, though it varies from person to person). Growth plates are important because they create bone and so determine its size and shape. Damage to the growth plate can interfere with bone growth and cause problems in later life due to deformity, short bone length, nerve damage or arthritis.

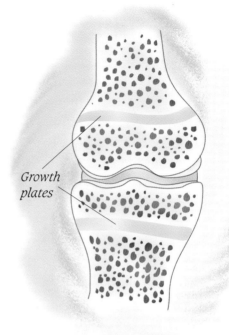

Growth plates

The types of sports injury that can damage growth plates in children are the same types that cause sprains or ligament damage (see Chapter 4) in adults and older adolescents. Growth plate injuries can be caused by overuse (in sports such as gymnastics and baseball) as well as by trauma (more common in contact sports such as judo or American football).

Growth plate injuries are treated by immobilizing the affected limb until the injury heals. This must be followed by strengthening exercises. Occasionally, manipulation (moving the damaged sections of bone) or surgery is needed to make sure that the bone heals in the correct position.

Growth plates

Damage to the growth plates in the long bones is a particular danger for young people taking part in sport.

Overuse and trauma

Sports injuries can usually be divided into two categories:

Traumatic injuries *are caused instantly by unusual force or by contact with a person or object. They can occur when you slip, trip, fall or collide with something or someone.*

Overuse injuries *develop slowly over time. They are caused if you place excessive strain on a muscle, tendon, joint or ligament, by performing the same movement over and over again.*

Women and sport

Women are involved in sport more than ever before. Many years ago it was commonly thought that women needed to train at a lower level than men. Research has not confirmed this idea. It appears that women are able to train and, increasingly, compete at a similar level to men. The only injury that affects women more than men is damage to the anterior cruciate ligament in the knee. Women between the ages of 15 and 25 seem to be three to four times more likely than men to sustain this form of injury. The reason for this seems to be that women tend to use their leg muscles in a different way to men and, when they jump, they tend to land on a flat foot rather than their toes. It is thought that the number of women with knee injuries could be reduced by improved training techniques.

Male genitalia are at greater risk of injury than female, for the obvious reason that their position in the body is much more exposed. There is no bar to women participating in sport before, during or after menstruation. Women who experience particularly painful or heavy periods should consult their doctor, as there are many treatments available to reduce their impact.

Some female athletes are very thin (often runners, dancers or gymnasts). If their diet is not nutritious enough, they may experience 'athletic amenorrhoea' – which involves periods becoming infrequent or disappearing altogether. This is due to disrupted hormone production and can be treated by adjusting the diet. Long-term amenorrhoea can lead to an increased risk of osteoporosis when older.

Basic sporting safety

Taking time to check that you are safe before you begin to take part in a sport can reduce your likelihood of injury. First you need to make sure that you are in good physical condition to play. You should not play if you are unwell, very tired or you have an injury.

Golden hat-trick
Marion Jones won gold medals in the 100m, 200m and 4x400m at the Sydney Olympics 2000.

It is very important to take 10 to 15 minutes to warm up and gently stretch your muscles before you start any sports session. A proper 'warm up' involves gentle stretching exercises, combined with exercises designed to get your joints and muscles mobile and ready for action. If you do not 'warm up' and prepare your body for physical activity, you run the risk of over-stretching and straining ligaments and muscles or even tearing them. A good warm-up routine gradually takes your body through the whole range of movements in a controlled manner and finishes with skill rehearsal, in which you practise the movements required by your specific sport. Then, when you come to repeat these movements during your sporting activity, your muscles and joints are primed to perform them in the correct way, and this reduces your risk of injury. Your coach will teach you the best warm-up routine for your sport.

Professional help

You should always seek a doctor's advice following a sporting injury, especially if you experience any of the following symptoms:

- *You are unable to carry on playing.*
- *You continue to find it more difficult to play a sport.*
- *You have a visible deformity of your arms or legs.*
- *You have severe pain from an injury that prevents you using an arm, leg, hand or foot.*
- *You experience continuing pain.*
- *You have a head injury.*

Getting ready

These sprinters are preparing for a training session with exercises to stretch their muscles.

You need to check that your equipment is in good order, and not becoming dangerously worn. It should also be the right size and weight for you. Your sports shoes should be in good condition, fit you properly and be appropriate for the sport you are undertaking. You should have the correct safety equipment, such as shin guards, helmet, face protector, body padding, genital protection for boys (often called a box), teeth guards, etc. It is also important to know how to use your sports equipment safely. A good coach will provide training and constant reminders about these factors.

'I love tennis. Out on the court it's just me, my opponent and hitting the ball.'
(Nicole, aged 15)

You need to know and keep to the rules of the sport in which you are participating. The rules of a sport are there to ensure fair play and to keep players as safe as possible. Everyone needs proper training to take part in sports. A qualified coach will encourage you to train for the sport so that you are in good physical condition when you take part and therefore less likely to be injured. Sports players who feel pressured to 'win at all costs' are more likely to become injured. Good coaches will also ensure that the sport remains fun and that it does not become overly competitive.

Safety summary

- ● *Do not play sport if you are unwell, over-tired or in pain.*
- ● *Make sure you are in good physical condition.*
- ● *Warm up for 10 to 15 minutes before starting to play.*
- ● *Wear the appropriate safety equipment for the sport.*
- ● *Make sure all equipment is in good condition and know how to use it properly.*
- ● *Know and keep to the rules of the game.*
- ● *Wear appropriate and well-fitting sports shoes.*
- ● *Always train with a properly qualified sports coach.*

2 Head and face injuries
Being on your guard

Sports with a high risk of head and facial injuries

Rugby	Skateboarding
American football	Hockey
Judo	Baseball
Boxing	Basketball
Wrestling	Cricket
Speed-skating	Soccer
Horse-riding	Lacrosse
Skiing	Golf
Snowboarding	Volleyball
Cycling	Tennis

Head injuries usually occur as a result of trauma (an accident) rather than from overuse. Slipping, tripping, falling or colliding can all cause injury to parts of your head, including your skull, eyes, ears, mouth, nose and cheekbones. Such accidents can result in broken bones (often called fractures) and internal or external bleeding.

Skull and brain injury

Injuries to the skull (the bones covering the top, sides and back of your head) are common, and most are not serious as the skull is very strong and designed to protect your brain.

Your brain is a very complex delicate organ. Damage to the brain can affect your whole body and, unlike other parts of your body, damaged brain tissue remains damaged. So any head injury, whether there is an obvious wound or not,

Punch drunk
Boxing is unique in the sporting world in that it involves repeated blows to the body and head.

needs to be treated with caution. Medical advice should be sought.

Your brain can be damaged by direct force, such as a blow to the head, or by indirect force, such as shaking. The force causes tiny blood vessels inside the brain to rupture and results in bleeding. Bleeding inside or around the brain can disrupt the way the brain works and increase the pressure inside the skull. This can cause headache, sickness and other symptoms, depending on which part of the brain is affected by the bleeding. For example, if the left part of the brain is affected, the person may have weakness in the right side of their body.

When just a few blood vessels are damaged and the bleeding is slight, causing mild bruising to the brain, the injury is called a concussion. This sort of injury is treated by rest and usually gets better in a few days. Severe bleeding inside the skull or brain can result in loss of consciousness, permanent brain damage or even death.

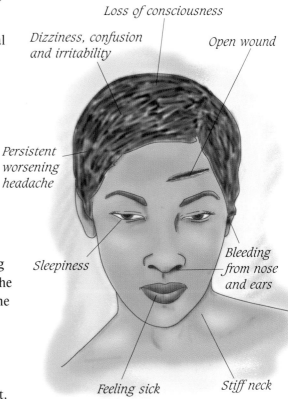

Loss of consciousness

Dizziness, confusion and irritability

Open wound

Persistent worsening headache

Sleepiness

Bleeding from nose and ears

Feeling sick and vomiting

Stiff neck

Head injuries

A head injury can cause a range of symptoms.

A doctor's view of boxing

'There is an on-going debate in the media as to whether boxing is so dangerous that it should be banned completely. Occasionally, repeated blows to a boxer's head can cause permanent brain damage or even death. Many people, me included, feel that all boxers are at risk of long-term brain damage. Often people give the example of the boxer Muhammad Ali, who has developed Parkinson's symptoms, which are thought to have been caused by his time in the ring. But some people feel that the evidence linking brain disorders like Parkinson's with repeated head injury in boxing is unclear. The groups that regulate professional boxing have acted to improve safety, by introducing longer gaps between fights for boxers who have been knocked out (i.e. lost consciousness), annual health checks and improved ringside medical attention. However, medical groups such as the British Medical Association feel that boxing is so dangerous that it should be banned.' (Mary, family doctor)

Treating skull and brain injuries

When someone has a head injury, the doctor will usually ask for an X-ray to check if any bones in the skull have been fractured. If the injury is severe, an operation may be needed to make sure that the skull bones are in the correct position to heal properly.

If the doctor thinks that there has been bleeding that may damage the brain, an operation will be necessary to remove the blood build-up. If the bleeding is only minor, the patient will usually be watched to ensure that their condition is not becoming worse and the blood is left to be reabsorbed naturally. This is a similar process to the way your body reabsorbs bruises on your skin.

'I crashed my bike last summer – bent the front wheel and got taken to hospital. They said I was lucky to get away with just concussion. I always wear my cycle helmet now.'
(Robert, aged 15, cyclist)

It can take weeks or months to recover from a severe head injury and you can be left with continuing problems such as tiredness, memory loss and difficulty concentrating. Sometimes people who have had a head injury go on to develop epilepsy. Recovery from minor concussions (brain bruises) is usually fairly easy and uncomplicated but can take several weeks.

Reducing the risk of head injury

Wearing a protective helmet reduces the risk of head injury. Head protection varies, depending on the sport, but is an essential piece of equipment in sports that carry a high risk of head injury such as downhill skiing, cycling, roller-skating, cricket and baseball.

Facial injuries

Injuries to the face and cheekbones can occur in many sports, but they are a particular risk for those playing ice hockey and hockey (because of the risk from flying pucks and sticks), those playing rugby, soccer, baseball and American football, horse-riders, downhill skiers and snowboarders. These injuries include bruising, open wounds (where the upper layers of the skin are damaged enough to cause bleeding) and fractures.

Heat exhaustion

Athletes who participate in sports during hot weather are at risk of heat exhaustion. Sports where this is likely include tennis, American football, long-distance running and basketball. Heat exhaustion is also more common in younger athletes, as they are often smaller and not as strong as adults.

The symptoms of heat exhaustion can be nausea, vomiting and eventually loss of consciousness and death. Heat exhaustion can cause brain damage. It is caused by your body losing water through sweating, combined with a raised body temperature.

Heat exhaustion is preventable if you gradually get used to playing in hotter environments, do not play in the heat of the day between 11 am and 3 pm, and make sure that you keep drinking lots while you are playing. We can lose more than 2 kg of body weight in fluid, through perspiration, for every hour of vigorous exercise, and this needs to be replaced. A good way of telling if you are getting dehydrated (your body is becoming dangerously low on water) is to look at the colour of your urine. If it is a strong yellow colour you need more fluid. It should be a clear, very pale yellow.

Unless a wound to the face is superficial (only affecting the surface layer of the skin), it should always be seen by a doctor as it can be difficult to tell whether the facial bones have been damaged or not. Fractures of the facial bones can result in teeth being out of alignment, and pain when opening or closing the mouth or trying to chew. It is very important that facial injuries are properly assessed, as fractures that are missed can result in long-term pain when eating and facial disfigurement.

First aid for bleeding wounds

You should always wear surgical or rubber gloves when dealing with a bleeding wound. Diseases such as HIV and hepatitis can be spread by contact with infected blood, so wearing protective gloves is a vital routine safety precaution.

For wounds that are bleeding profusely:

1 *Remove any clothing over the wound and check to see if the wound is dirty or has anything stuck in it. Do not try to remove anything you find, but make sure that the patient is seen by a qualified first aider or a doctor for further treatment.*

2 *Place a clean pad over the wound and apply pressure with your fingers.*

3 *Maintain the pressure and, if possible, raise the injured area to reduce bleeding.*

4 *Bandage the pad firmly in place, but make sure that you do not bandage so tightly that you cut off the blood supply.*

5 *If bleeding is severe, keep the patient lying down.*

Injuries should always be properly checked out by a first aider or a qualified medical practitioner. If bleeding is severe, call for an ambulance.

Open facial wounds (cuts, grazes and lacerations) need to be treated with care. These wounds are often dirty, because of contact with muddy equipment or a hard gritty floor (a particular problem for athletes). They need careful cleaning to ensure that no pieces of grit remain and to reduce the risk of infection. Deep wounds may need suturing (stitches) to keep the edges of the wound in alignment and reduce scarring. Long-term problems from facial wounds are rare, but can include wound infections from dirt, nerve damage, disfigurement from scarring, and dental problems.

Nose injuries

Most people associate a broken nose with boxing, but nose injuries can also occur in any sport where facial injury is a risk. The nose is more commonly injured than the cheekbones, as the nose sticks out and therefore tends to hit the ground or flying missile first, protecting the rest of the face from damage. Injuries to the nose often cause

Nosebleed

Usually, a nosebleed can be treated successfully by firmly pinching the soft part of the nose, below the bridge, whilst leaning forwards for five to ten minutes. If bleeding does not stop after half an hour, medical advice should be sought.

bruising and bleeding. An injury can also cause a fracture of the nasal bones at the top of the nose, or of the strong cartilage that separates your nostrils.

Most of your nose is made up of soft tissue and cartilage, with a small ridge of bone at the top. It is primarily used for warming and filtering the air you breathe and for registering different smells. Your nose has a large network of fine blood vessels and these are easily damaged.

Fractures of the nasal bone and cartilage can result in the nose being obviously out of line. Also the person may have difficulty breathing through their nose, and this needs medical attention. Nose fractures are often accompanied by prolonged nose bleeding. Any nosebleed that continues after 30 minutes of continuous pinching below the bridge of the nose, as shown in the photograph, needs to be assessed by a medical practitioner. Long-term problems following nasal fractures that are not properly treated include a misshapen nose and difficulty breathing through the nostrils.

'I thought face guards were a waste of time until I was smashed by a stick in an away match. Three weeks of only being able to drink through a straw while my jaw was wired changed my mind. I never play without a guard now.'
(Mark, aged 16, hockey player)

Ear injuries

Injuries to the ear area, which may occur in sports such as boxing, wrestling and rugby, can cause swelling and bleeding in the cartilage of the outer ear. This can result in 'cauliflower ear', where the ear becomes permanently deformed.

Other sports that can affect the ears include swimming, surfing, diving and water polo. 'Swimmer's ear' (which can also occur in athletes) is an infection that occurs in the outer ear canal. It is sometimes called *Otitis externa* and occurs when water or perspiration in the ear canal provides ideal growing conditions for bacteria and fungi. People swimming in polluted or dirty water are at risk, but so are those who swim in clean, chlorinated pools. Chlorine can dry the ear canal and disrupts the natural protection from infection that is provided by earwax. Signs of ear infection include ear pain, occasionally slight fever, discharge from the ear canal, and temporary loss of hearing on the side affected.

'I've had the occasional ear infection from swimming, but other than that I've been lucky. I wear ear plugs now to stop the chlorine in the pool irritating my ears.' (Shona, aged 15)

You should check with your family doctor if you suspect you have an ear infection. Sometimes these infections require medication to help them get better. It is wise to avoid getting water in your ear canal while you have an ear infection and for three weeks following recovery, to prevent the problem returning.

Eye injuries

In the USA, sports and recreational activities cause more than 31,000 eye injuries every year. Corneal abrasion is the commonest form of eye injury. This is a condition where the cornea, the outer surface of the eye, is scratched. The condition is painful but not usually dangerous and can easily be caused by another player's fingernail. Basketball and netball players are at particular risk of this type of injury.

'I got hit in the eye by a cricket ball once. We were playing an inter-school match and the glare from the sun made me misjudge the ball. The optician said I was lucky not to do more damage. The black eye lasted for weeks.' (Adrian, aged 13)

Impact eye injuries occur when an object (such as a ball, elbow, fist or racquet) comes into contact with the eye and causes compression. This can result in bruising and/or bleeding around the eye (causing a 'black eye'), or inside the eye. Bleeding inside the eye can cause temporary loss of vision, and this can become permanent if the injury is severe. Bleeding inside the eye is quite difficult to diagnose, so it is essential that eye injuries are assessed by an ophthalmologist.

Another common injury occurs when a foreign body pierces the eye. This can occur when someone's spectacles shatter, or occasionally when a piece of sharp gravel flies off a playing surface. People who need to wear glasses should wear impact-resistant ones for playing sport. These types of injuries can be severe and can potentially cause blindness. Prompt professional treatment is always required.

Eye patch

The most common eye injury is corneal abrasion where the cornea (covering of the eye) is scratched. This can be caused by sand or gravel from the playing field or an opponent's fingernail. The eye feels gritty and irritated. Treatment is to rest the eye, sometimes by wearing a patch. The condition usually gets better in 24 to 48 hours, though occasionally antibiotic eye-drops are needed to aid healing.

Black eye
Bruising around the eye is often called a 'black eye'. Eye injuries need to be checked by a doctor to ensure there is no hidden damage.

Detached retina

Detached retina is a rare but serious injury to the eye, which can occur after a blow to the head, or a fall. The retina lines the inside of the back of your eye and is an essential part of the mechanism of vision. Detached retinas are difficult to diagnose and anyone who has limited or impaired vision following an impact should be examined by an ophthalmologist, as this condition can result in blindness if it is not treated.

All eye injuries should be properly examined by an ophthalmologist. But the best way to deal with eye injuries is to prevent them in the first place. Eye specialists recommend that everyone taking part in sport should wear protective eye guards. People who participate in racquet sports, such as tennis, badminton, squash and lacrosse, basketball players and those involved in collision sports such as football, rugby and hockey are at particular risk.

Mouth injuries

Injuries affecting the teeth, cheeks and tongue can occur in any sporting accidents involving slips, trips or falls. Mouth injuries are often very painful, as the mouth has a very good nerve supply and is therefore a sensitive area. It is very common for children and young people to damage or knock out a tooth, and in approximately a quarter of such cases, the injury occurs during a sporting activity. Sports in which people are more at risk of these types of injury include contact or collision sports, such as hockey, football, rugby and basketball, sports with a hard ball, such as cricket, and those with equipment like lacrosse.

'Sometimes teeth are broken or cracked by impacts with sticks or balls, or by slips, trips and falls on the sports pitch. If they are adult teeth, we have to insert caps or crowns to improve the appearance.' (Alan, dentist)

If you damage or knock out a tooth, you should see a dentist as a matter of emergency. Teeth that are knocked out can often be successfully re-implanted. It has to be done with speed, as the delicate cells on the root of the tooth, which anchor it to the jaw, are easily damaged.

Tackling safety
Mouth guards are worn to protect the teeth in contact and collision sports.

Many dentists say that, as long as the knocked-out tooth is clean and undamaged, you should implant it back into the jaw immediately, ensuring that it is the right way round; and then seek a dentist's advice. However, this should only be attempted with adult teeth. Attempting to re-implant a baby tooth may result in damage to the developing adult tooth underneath it. If you are unable to reinsert the tooth, you should keep it moist and see a dentist straight away.

Mouth injuries can be prevented by the use of a mouth guard (sometimes called a gum shield). These are commonly used in boxing, wrestling, American football, rugby and ice hockey or wherever the athlete needs extra protection or is at increased risk of injury.

Sports focus: skateboarding

Skateboarding is an increasingly popular sport. However, as with any sport where you move at speed (including cycling, skating and skiing), there is a high risk of injury. Skateboarders are most at risk of fractures, especially to the arms and wrists, and head injuries, particularly when practising stunts. In the USA, 50,000 skateboarding accidents require emergency treatment every year.

It is suggested that children under 5 should never ride a skateboard and that children between 6 and 10 should only do so with adult supervision. The ability to balance, reaction times, coordination and skill level all tend to be less well developed in young people and this makes them more likely to fall and be injured while skateboarding. It is estimated that 60% of skate-boarding injuries happen to people below the age of 15.

Skateboarders should take these precautions.

Environment
❶ Always skate on smooth paths, away from traffic and pedestrians.
❶ Don't wear headphones when skating.

Equipment
❶ Make sure your skateboard is in good working order, able to run smoothly and strong enough to take your weight.
❶ Make sure you do not have any hard or sharp objects in your pockets, which could injure you if you fall.

'I get a real thrill from skateboarding. You have to play it safe though – it's not cool to break your neck.' (Jed, aged 14)

❶ Wear good-quality, properly-fitting safety equipment including gloves and wrist guards, knee and elbow pads and shoes that do not slip.

Safety helmets

❶ These should be worn flat and low on your head, with the bottom parallel to the ground.

❶ They should have side straps that fit with a V around each ear, and an adjustable buckle that fastens securely under your chin.

❶ There should be adjustable pads inside the helmet to ensure that it does not move when you shake your head.

❶ The helmet should be replaced when it becomes worn, after an impact, when you outgrow it, or every five years – whichever comes first.

Training

❶ Make sure you know how to stop properly, slow and turn and how to fall safely.

❶ If you feel you are losing your balance, crouch down on the skateboard so there is not so far to fall. Try to land on the fleshy parts of your body and relax and roll as you fall.

❶ Make sure you are in good physical condition.

❶ Warm up before you start.

❶ Be careful with tricks and jumps. Improve your skills in small stages.

Preventing head and face injuries

Your coach or trainer should give you specific advice about injury prevention in your sport.

◉ *Make sure your equipment is in good condition and is safe.*

◉ *Ensure that the playing surface and general environment are safe. (Check for uneven or slippery surfaces and loose material.)*

◉ *Make sure that all players know, understand and abide by the rules of the game.*

◉ *Wear appropriate head protection.*

◉ *Wear appropriate eye protection – if you wear glasses, ensure that they are shatterproof.*

◉ *Wear appropriate mouth protection or gum shields.*

◉ *Wear appropriate face shields (particularly for baseball, cricket and American football).*

◉ *Wear appropriate ear protection (e.g. strapping in rugby).*

◉ *Find a good trainer with appropriate qualifications and first aid training.*

◉ *Do not take unnecessary risks.*

3 Chest and torso injuries
Reducing the impact

Most injuries to the chest, abdomen and groin areas are impact injuries. They can cause bruising, fractures of the rib cage and open wounds.

Chest and rib injuries

The pectoral muscles of your chest and rib area are at risk from direct hits, or from wrenching and blocking tactics in combat sports such as judo and karate. Injury of this sort can cause severe internal bleeding and can be fatal, particularly for children, who have less well-developed muscle and rib protection. However, more commonly, chest injuries result in bruising, muscle or tendon strains or tears, and broken ribs. All these can also be caused by pressure changes inside your rib cage. For example, if you are using a vertical leg press exercise machine, the increased air pressure when you take a deep breath in before pushing your legs up against the weights can be enough to injure your ribs or your chest muscles.

Sports most likely to cause chest and torso injuries

Soccer	Badminton
American football	Tennis
Hockey	Baseball
Ice hockey	Discus
Rugby	Javelin
Karate	Handball
Judo	Weightlifting
Wrestling	Hurdling
Volleyball	High-jumping

Internal injuries

Impact injuries to the chest and abdomen can result in severe damage to the internal organs. However, it is much more common for such injuries only to damage the bones and muscles that protect the organs.

Sudden death can occur if the heart is damaged by broken ribs

Ruptured liver caused by injury to the abdomen can be fatal

Ruptured spleen caused by injury to the abdomen can be fatal

The muscles between your ribs and over your chest are also at risk from overuse injuries. Sports that involve repetitive overarm movements, such as tennis, badminton, and pitching in cricket or baseball, have an increased risk of overuse injuries in this area.

The pain from a chest injury, such as fractured ribs, can make it difficult to take a deep breath and cough properly. This results in difficulty clearing mucus from your lungs and therefore increases the risk of developing a chest infection.

Broken ribs where the bones are not pushed out of normal position are usually left to heal on their own. The ribs normally heal in about three weeks, but they should not be put under any strain, as this can delay healing by preventing the bones knitting together properly. It is a good idea to practise taking deep breaths every hour while you are recovering, to prevent chest infections. Once you have recovered from a rib cage injury, you need to return to full activities slowly. You may have lost some of your muscle strength and flexibility and you need to build this up again before you carry on your sporting activities as before. Otherwise, you risk injuring yourself again.

First aid for bruising

Bruises are caused by bleeding inside your body (usually into skin or muscle tissue). This causes swelling, pain and discolouration that is visible through the skin. Bruising can develop very slowly and may take days to appear fully. Bruising that appears quickly is most responsive to first aid treatment. All injuries need to be assessed by a qualified first aider, as bruising can be a sign of underlying injury, such as a fracture. Bruising on the abdomen can also be a sign of internal bleeding.

Bruising usually responds well to simple treatment:
1 Raise the affected area and support it in a comfortable position.
2 Apply a cold compress to the area (for example, a bag of frozen peas or ice cubes wrapped in a wet wrung-out towel to prevent ice burns). This causes the blood vessels near the surface of the skin to contract, which slows or stops the bleeding that is producing the bruise and reduces the swelling.

Sports focus: Hockey

Hockey is played by men and women in 132 countries and is the second most popular team sport in the world, after soccer. Hockey players use sticks to hit a ball; the game also involves tackling other players to gain possession of the ball and hitting the ball a long way down the field at speed, to prevent interception. All these factors put hockey players at risk of injury. It has been estimated that 15% of all professional hockey players are injured during the playing season. Ice hockey players have an even greater risk of injury. In Australia, one study estimated that 50% of all hockey injuries occurred to players in the 10–19 age group. The most serious injuries from hockey come from being struck by the stick or the ball. This can affect any part of the body, including the chest and abdomen. The most common injuries in hockey include sprains, strains, bruises, lacerations and fractures.

'As a goalie, I'm very glad of the extra padding. It takes guts to stand in front of a hockey ball flying at high speed. I've had some impressive bruises.'
(Li, aged 14, ice hockey goalie)

Sensible safety precautions for playing hockey include:

Good preparation

❶ Players need to be fit and well before they start to play.
❶ You should always warm up and practise moves for 10 to 15 minutes before a game.

Safety equipment

❶ Goalkeepers should wear a protective helmet and face guard.
❶ American safety advice suggests that all hockey and ice hockey players should wear protective helmets and face guards.
❶ All players should wear shin guards and mouth guards.
❶ American safety advice suggests that all players should also wear shoulder pads, elbow pads, hip pads, tendon pads, gloves and padded hockey trousers. This is not common practice in all countries.

'I love hockey. It's a great team sport – we're all great mates.'
(Amy, aged 13)

Goalkeeper

Goalkeepers must protect every part of their body.

- Male players should wear athletic supporters to protect the genital and groin area.
- Good-quality footwear should be worn, appropriate for pitch conditions.

Good technique

- Properly qualified coaches can advise on and monitor skill development, which can reduce the risk of injury.
- Training should concentrate on good ball handling technique and safe use of the hockey stick.
- All players should be aware of and keep to the rules of the game.
- Good referees are needed to ensure that play remains safe and fair.
- Young players should be encouraged to play Minkey (played on a quarter pitch with six players a side) or Half-field hockey (played on half a field with seven players a side), in order to develop their skill before progressing to full pitch play.

Environment

- The pitch should be inspected to make sure that there are no areas that could cause slips, trips or falls.
- Equipment should be inspected to make sure that it is safe. Hockey sticks should be sound, free from cracks and splinters.
- Hockey matches should not be played in extreme weather conditions such as severe heat, cold or storms.

4 Back injuries
Preserving the vital link

Sports with a risk of spinal injury

Diving	Weightlifting
Horse-riding	Golf
Cycling	Rugby
Rowing	American
Tennis	football
Badminton	Judo
Squash	Snowboarding

Your spine is made up of 26 bones called vertebrae: 7 cervical (neck), 12 thoracic (chest area), 5 lumbar (lower back), and the sacral and coccygeal vertebrae (the sacrum and coccyx) which extend down to your bottom. Between each vertebra and the next is a flexible plate of cartilage, called a spinal disc. The discs protect the bones and allow limited flexibility, and act as a shock absorber to prevent damage to the spinal bones.

The spinal column supports the weight of your head and body and protects the fragile nerve supply (the spinal cord) that runs through the spinal canal to your brain. It is flexible enough to allow you to bend and move. Attached to the spine is a network of ligaments and muscles, which enable you to lift heavy loads and which provide the force for you to bend, stand and move. Back pain and back problems are very common: over 80% of people experience some form of back pain during their lifetime.

Spinal cord injuries

Fractures to the bones of the spine or severe knocks can damage the bundle of nerve fibres (the spinal cord) that

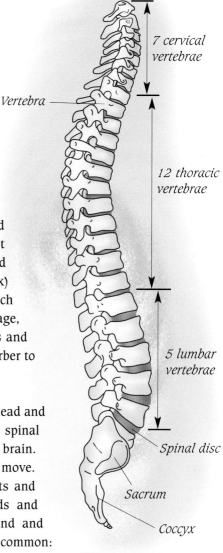

7 cervical vertebrae

Vertebra

12 thoracic vertebrae

5 lumbar vertebrae

Spinal disc

Sacrum

Coccyx

Bones of the spine
Each bone making up the spine is called a vertebra.

pass through the spinal canal. This can have serious consequences. The spinal cord carries the nerve connections between your brain and every part of your body. If a connection is disrupted (by being compressed by a slipped disc) or broken, the brain is unable to control the activity of the body below the break. Nerve fibres do not heal in the same way as skin, muscle or bone. Once they are badly damaged, they cannot be repaired. The higher up the spine the damage takes place, the greater the area of body affected. For example, if you fracture your lumbar spine and it affects the spinal canal, you may become paralysed in your feet or legs. If you fracture your cervical spine, your whole body can be left paralysed. Christopher Reeve (who starred in the film *Superman*) became paralysed from the neck down after fracturing his neck in a horse-riding accident.

Mostly male

50% of spinal cord injuries occur in young people aged 15–24. Of these, 82% are male.

Think first

'On holiday, when I was 14, a group of friends were daring each other to jump into a rocky cove from the cliff. Some of the others did it and were fine, but I hit a rock under the water. I'm paralysed from the waist down now. Of course I wish I'd never done it. But if I can just stop someone else being the sort of idiot I was, I'll have done some good. If I'd only thought for a minute then. You should never jump into unknown water. In fact, I would say only dive into purpose-built diving pools. Don't run and dive. Make sure your path is clear and practise carefully. Don't dive from cliffs, rooftops, balconies or ledges and never dive alone. I am only alive today because my friends were there to pull me out. My main message is: take care, you only have one pair of legs.' (Aaron, aged 18)

Thankfully, spinal injuries are rare. However, some sports have a higher risk of such injuries, including diving, horse-riding and contact sports, particularly American football where some tackles are performed by running into people head first. Taking proper precautions and wearing head protection can prevent many of these injuries.

Under normal circumstances, your spine is very strong and resistant to injury. However, any movement that puts your spine under abnormal pressure can injure it. This can be a sudden injury (for example, when a weightlifter is lifting a weight beyond his capacity) or an injury that develops over time (such as when a tennis or badminton player repeatedly twists awkwardly when serving).

Muscle and ligament injuries

The muscles of your back can be damaged by over-stretching, over-contracting, or twisting them. This is one of the reasons why sports professionals perform warm-up exercises for at least 15 minutes before they start play. Muscles that have not been through the warm-up process (where you gradually practise the movements that you will be expecting your body to perform during the sport action) are thought to be at greater risk of this form of injury.

Your mid spine can be injured by awkward twisting movements, such as lifting a boat out of the water, or by repetitive twisting movements, such as practising a particular tennis stroke. Injuries to the muscles and ligaments attached to your mid spine can cause pain in the back of the chest. However, pain in this area can also be caused by an illness of a structure inside your chest, such as your lungs or heart, or by referred pain from your liver or stomach. Referred pain is pain in one part of the body, due to something that is happening in a different area of the body. You should always get persistent pain checked out by a doctor.

Emergency

If you think someone has injured their spine, it is vital that you do not move them and that you get medical assistance quickly. Long-term consequences of spinal injury can include paralysis and even death.

'I thought I'd got a back injury from basketball. I had this dull aching pain in my back. Mum made me go to the doctor and it turned out I had a kidney infection that needed antibiotic treatment. I was glad I'd seen the doctor – it could have got worse.' (Alex, aged 14)

If you damage the cartilage that forms the joint between two spinal bones, the muscles surrounding the joint may go into spasm. This means that the muscles become very stiff, to prevent any movement that may cause further damage and to provide support for the damaged joint while it repairs. If you then force a movement from muscles that are in spasm, you risk tearing the muscle fibres and further damaging the joint. The lesson from this is not to continue if you are in pain, as you risk making the injury worse.

Scheuermann's disease

In this rare disease, which can affect boys (mostly) between the ages of 12 and 15, the vertebrae fail to grow properly and this causes upper back pain. The pain is often triggered by an injury and is worst when you bend forwards or backwards and after sport. It closely resembles a normal sports injury and doctors often become aware of the condition when someone has a sports injury that does not get better. Scheuermann's disease can cause the development of a hunch (a deformity of the spine where one side of the upper back is higher than the other). In severe cases, the sufferer may have to stop sporting activities and wear a brace to protect their spine. In mild cases, individuals may be able to continue sport. It is often treated by strengthening and mobilizing exercises.

Against the flow

Rowers can be at risk of back injury if they always row on the same side and when lifting the boat in and out of the water.

Spondylolysis

This is a stress fracture (see Chapter 5) of the lower part of the spine. If other members of your family have the condition, you are at an increased risk of developing it, as you can inherit a genetic tendency to it. However, it can also be caused by certain types of activity. Divers who arch their back while diving have an approximately 60% chance of acquiring the condition, which causes lower back pain. It frequently occurs just after an adolescent growth spurt. Spondylolysis can require the sufferer to wear a corset and may require surgery.

Vertebral disc damage

The discs of cartilage between the bones of your spine are designed to absorb impact and protect the spinal bones from damage. Rowers who always row on one side of the boat, weightlifters, participants in combat sports and those who play contact sports such as American football or rugby are at particular risk. The danger of damage increases as you get older, as the outer casing of the discs begins to degenerate slowly after the age of 25 years. If the discs become damaged, then the outer covering can crack and the disc itself may protrude from the spine and put pressure onto the spinal cord. This can cause severe pain and requires specialist treatment. After an injury like this it is extremely important to regain good strength and mobility in your spine before you go back to your sport, as repeated injuries of this nature can cause long-term pain and disability.

Contact sports and non-contact sports

Contact sports	Non-contact sports
Boxing	Baseball
Hockey	Basketball
American football	Cycling
Soccer	Diving
Ice hockey	Track events
Lacrosse	Jumping events
Judo	Throwing events
Karate	Gymnastics
Rugby	Ice skating
Wrestling	Rowing
	Skiing
	Snowboarding
	Tennis
	Badminton
	Volleyball

Lower spine injuries

Injuries to the lower spine are very common, particularly as people get older. Injuries to this area tend to be due to poor lifting technique, poor sitting or standing posture, lifting weights beyond your capacity, or overuse. Injuries to this area of your back are more likely if you play when tired or sick. They are also more common in sports that combine twisting movements with lifting movements. This includes sports such as rowing, judo, rugby and American football.

A lower spine injury can often be felt as a mild gnawing pain that gradually increases. The pain may be made worse by certain movements. It may also continue to hurt when you lie down or turn over at night. If nerve compression is involved, you may experience pain down your legs, or tingling and numbness in your legs.

Nerve compression

Because the spine contains the main nerve connections between your brain and the rest of your body, damage to the bones of your spine or compression of those bones can cause pain or loss of feeling in other parts of your body. For example, if you have an injury to the vertebrae of your neck, the swelling and muscle spasm from the injury may trap one of the nerves coming out of your spine and this will be experienced as pain or tingling in one of your arms, or your fingers. Lower back injuries may cause compression of the sciatic nerve, which connects your brain to your legs. This can cause pain, tingling and numbness in one of your legs. If the nerve is severely compressed, then the pain may extend down the whole of the leg and may even affect bowel and bladder control.

Nerve compression can be treated by rest and manipulation (by a physiotherapist or osteopath). Occasionally a doctor will prescribe medication, which reduces the spasm in the muscle in order to relieve pain.

'Sometimes I get a tingling pain in my fingers, which can make it difficult to write. The doctor says it's due to a trapped nerve in my neck from practising serving. My coach and physiotherapist have worked out a training regime for me that reduces the strain on my neck and we work on positions that don't cause the problem.' (Su lin, aged 15, tennis player)

Preventing spinal injuries

Preventing back and neck injuries in sport is mostly a matter of common sense. The main causes of spinal injuries are collisions or overuse. Therefore, all the general issues for safety in sport (see Chapter 1) should be observed, with particular attention to technique and fitness to play.

Many sports require competitors to wear head protection. Head protection can also protect the vulnerable neck area from compression injuries, though its use can be controversial. Some trainers and competitors feel that head protection can make players feel less vulnerable to injury and so they take more risks. Others feel that although head protection can reduce traumatic injury, it may increase the likelihood of generalized brain injury because of the shaking caused when something hits the helmet. However, the general consensus is that head protection is valuable and can help prevent head and neck injuries.

Sports focus: Judo

Judo is a martial art developed from the ancient martial art of ju-jitsu in 1882. Judo was introduced to the Olympic Games in 1964 and is practised by millions of people around the world. It involves learning how to defend yourself against a potential aggressor with the minimum of effort and risk.

The injury risk associated with judo is similar to that of other martial arts such as karate, kung fu, tae kwon do and ju-jitsu. Most martial arts are high-energy activities that can help build strength, flexibility and agility. Any activity that involves a combat situation is obviously risky. The risk of injury in martial arts is higher, the older you get. Children tend to be less prone to injury in this type of sport. This is partly to do with good training techniques and partly because younger children are not allowed to perform the more difficult manoeuvres until they are ready physically and

'In judo, you learn how to defend yourself and it is great for flexibility. You have to be careful of your back and head though. Luckily I haven't had any bad injuries yet.'
(Sylvie, aged 16)

mentally. Children are also lighter and so fall less heavily. The majority of traumatic injuries to people under 17 in martial arts are injuries to the arms and shoulders (boys) and head and neck area (girls). Overuse injuries to the spine are more likely for adults than those under 17.

The best way to reduce the likelihood of injury whilst participating in martial arts activities is to:

Ready for action
Young people under the age of 17 are less likely than adults to be injured during a judo combat.

❶ Focus on enjoying the sport rather than on winning. It is more important to build up good technique than to push yourself too hard, which increases your chance of injury.
❶ Before you start a training programme, make sure you are strong and healthy enough to participate safely.
❶ Make sure your trainer is properly qualified to teach the martial art you are learning
❶ Do not play through pain. If it hurts, stop. If you are injured, get it properly assessed and follow your doctor's advice. Do not return to play until the injury has healed properly.
❶ Make sure that someone trained in first aid is present at all training sessions and competitions.

First aid for muscle and ligament injuries – the RICE formula

Muscle, tendon and ligament injuries are perhaps the most common sports injuries. The RICE formula is a very effective treatment for them, particularly for injuries to the legs and arms. However the RICE formula can be adapted for treating muscle and ligament injuries wherever they occur in the body. Muscular back injuries, for example, benefit from rest and ice.

R stands for REST. Resting the affected area does not mean that you have to spend the day in bed. To rest an ankle following an injury, you may be given crutches to help you get around. To rest an arm, you may need to wear a sling for a few days.

Research shows that recovery is faster if, once the pain has eased, the injured area is used again as soon as possible. It is wise to have a doctor's or physiotherapist's advice about this, as different injuries need different periods of rest and different exercise regimes. However, in general, you should begin to use the affected area as soon as you can, as long as the activity you are doing does not cause pain.

It is wise to keep up your general fitness, and so your physiotherapist or doctor may advise you to take up another form of training (such as stationary cycling, Pilates, or swimming) that does not put pressure on the injured area. You may also be advised to do stretching exercises, followed (as recovery progresses) by strengthening exercises. This ensures that the injured area returns to full strength and reduces your risk of sustaining the injury again. Many sports medicine professionals feel that it is unwise to return to play until you have regained 80–90% of the strength in the affected side.

I stands for ICE. *The application of an ice bag (a bag of frozen peas wrapped in a wet, wrung-out cloth in order to prevent ice burns) reduces the amount of swelling around the injured area. This works because the coldness makes the capillaries (tiny blood vessels) shrink, reducing blood flow to the area. The ice needs to be applied for at least 20 minutes, preferably with the area raised, every two hours for the first two days following an injury, although three times a day is acceptable. Heat packs can make the injury feel more comfortable, but should not be used for the first 48 hours as they can encourage swelling and bleeding.*

C stands for COMPRESSION. *The affected area should be compressed, and elastic or crêpe bandage is most effective. Make sure the bandage is not too tight. It should be checked every hour to ensure that toes or fingers are still warm and pink and that no sensations of tingling are felt. Tight bandaging cuts off the blood supply to the affected area, which can result in more damage. But firm bandaging can help to prevent further swelling and aid recovery.*

E stands for ELEVATION. *Elevating (raising) the affected area also reduces swelling by using gravity to pull body fluids away from the injured area.*

Always get injuries checked out by a doctor to ensure that there are no hidden injuries and to get good advice for a quick recovery.

5 Leg and foot injuries
Keeping in prime condition

Injury points
Different types of injury occur to different parts of the leg.

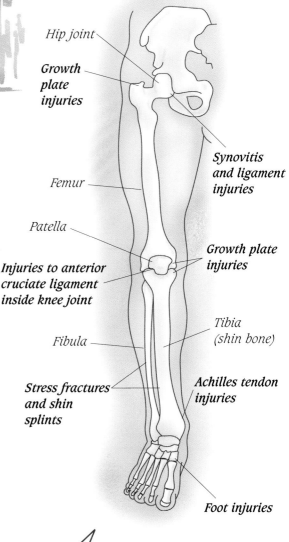

Hip joint

Growth plate injuries

Femur

Patella

Injuries to anterior cruciate ligament inside knee joint

Fibula

Stress fractures and shin splints

Synovitis and ligament injuries

Growth plate injuries

Tibia (shin bone)

Achilles tendon injuries

Foot injuries

Each of your legs contains three main bones: the femur (from hip joint to knee) and the tibia and fibula (from knee to ankle). They are held together by the knee joint, which is made up of cartilage and a small piece of bone called the patella, which protects the joint. The bones and knee joint are connected by muscles and ligaments, which enable your legs to move and support the weight of your body. Each foot has 26 bones and approximately 30 ligaments connecting the muscles of the foot and leg, to enable the foot to move and function properly.

Your legs and feet are under pressure during normal activity, as they carry the load of your body when standing, walking, running, bending, kneeling, climbing stairs and getting up from sitting or lying down. When you play sport, the load can be greatly increased. Actions such as kicking a ball can produce tremendous force through your legs and feet, as can jumping, dancing and activities such as cycling and skiing.

Exercise is vital to keep your feet and legs in prime condition and able to meet the demands of normal life. However, any injury or problems with your legs and feet can be very disabling. A small injury to your foot can make it difficult or painful to walk and can have a big impact on the way you live your life. So it is very important to take care of your legs and take action to prevent injuries.

Hip and thigh injuries

Pain around the hip and the top of the thigh can be due to joint, muscle or ligament injuries. However, it can be a sign of problems with the internal organs of the pelvis, such as appendicitis, urinary tract infections, gynaecological problems and hernias. In children and adolescents, hip pain can be caused by Perthes disease, growth plate injuries, or synovitis.

Perthes disease occurs between the ages of 3 and 11 and affects the shape of the hip joint. The disease is rare and treatable, but recovery can take a long time. Growth plate injuries at the neck of the femur (where the hip bone becomes the hip joint) can occasionally affect people (mostly boys) between the ages of 11 and 16. Synovitis is inflammation of the hip joint tissues. This occurs mainly in children under 10 years old. Although it is painful and needs to be investigated by an orthopaedic specialist to ensure that it is not confused with any other condition, it usually gets better without any intervention.

'I've damaged ligaments and muscles in my hips and legs, but they have always got better with rest and ice packs. Whilst I'm recovering, I do Pilates, which enables you to exercise certain muscles and rest others.'
(Holly, aged 17, dancer)

'My knees give me trouble occasionally, but I find that if I adjust the height of my saddle and the angle I am sitting at, I can avoid most problems. It's good to get advice before the problems get too bad.'
(Ainsley, aged 18, cyclist)

Lower leg injuries

Cramp is a very common lower leg problem, particularly during training in hot weather. Cramp is a sudden, severe pain caused by a muscle going into spasm. Why muscles do this is not very well understood. Some people seem to be more prone to cramp than others, but many sports experts believe that cramp is more likely if you do not have enough fluid in your body. So it is important to keep drinking during hot weather, and to slowly build up your tolerance of training in hot weather. Cramps in the calf muscle can be relieved by stretching the toes up towards the leg and massaging the muscle.

'Shin splints' is a general term for several injuries that cause pain in the lower leg. The membrane covering the tibia or fibula, where a tendon attaches, becomes inflamed and painful. The pain commonly occurs after running and, if it is ignored, it can result in a stress fracture. Treatment involves rest and anti-inflammatory drugs.

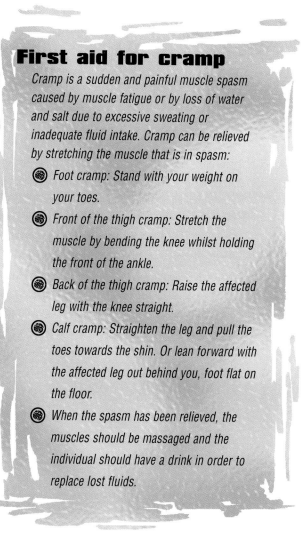

First aid for cramp

Cramp is a sudden and painful muscle spasm caused by muscle fatigue or by loss of water and salt due to excessive sweating or inadequate fluid intake. Cramp can be relieved by stretching the muscle that is in spasm:

- *Foot cramp: Stand with your weight on your toes.*
- *Front of the thigh cramp: Stretch the muscle by bending the knee whilst holding the front of the ankle.*
- *Back of the thigh cramp: Raise the affected leg with the knee straight.*
- *Calf cramp: Straighten the leg and pull the toes towards the shin. Or lean forward with the affected leg out behind you, foot flat on the floor.*
- *When the spasm has been relieved, the muscles should be massaged and the individual should have a drink in order to replace lost fluids.*

Ankle and foot injuries

Injuries to the muscles and ligaments of the ankle are very common and can usually be treated by observing the RICE formula (see pages 42-43). Basketball players are liable to foot and ankle injuries, because of the jumping and twisting involved in the game. These movements can result in a fracture of the fifth metatarsal bone in the foot.

Severs syndrome is similar to Osgood-Schlatter syndrome (see page 46) and affects children around 11 years of age. It involves inflammation of the growth plate in the heel. This stops being a problem once the growth plate has hardened at about age 13 in girls and 15 in boys. It is treated by rest, ice and using a rubber heel inside the shoe to protect the area.

The Achilles tendon is a tendon that runs up the back of the ankle and connects the muscles at the back of the leg to the heel. It can be torn or pulled or can become inflamed from overuse. Injuries to the Achilles tendon are very painful but usually respond well to the RICE formula. Anti-inflammatory medication may be needed. Complete ruptures of the Achilles tendon require surgical repair, followed by up to 12 weeks' recovery with the ankle immobilized in a plaster cast.

Snow sports
The legs are vulnerable to injury in skiing, as the feet are attached rigidly to the skis.

'I felt a snap'

'I was running down the field, nearly on the ball, when it was passed out to the sideline. I turned suddenly and my foot, instead of swivelling with my leg, stayed stuck in the mud. My knee came with me in the turn and I felt a snap. It was terrible. That face you see on the telly, when footballers fall down in agony, is not put on – it really hurts. I was stretchered off and the doc said I'd ruptured my Achilles tendon, which was really bad news. I've had some surgery to help it repair and now I'm trying to get back to normal. It's going to be a few months before I can play again, but I am determined to get back in the team.'
(Jordan, aged 15, soccer player)

Sports shoes

Properly-fitting sports shoes can help to prevent many sports injuries, especially those to the feet, ankles and legs, and can help you perform at your best. There are almost as many varieties of sports shoe as there are sports. You need shoes that provide support, flexibility and strength, depending on your sport. For example, for climbing, you would need flexible, supportive shoes that provide good grip. For football, you would need shoes that provide strong support and have studs underneath to provide grip and help prevent slips, trips and falls on wet or muddy pitches. For cycling, you may well need shoes with a cleat on the base to attach to the cycle pedals. A cleat is a moulded piece of metal or heavy-duty plastic that attaches a shoe to equipment. Likewise, skiers need special boots that attach to their skis.

Measuring up
For some sports you need shoes with studs or spikes. For others, like tennis, you need shoes with a smoother tread.

Shoes for running, walking, jogging or general athletics training need to have good shock absorption, to reduce the amount of pressure on your feet every time they hit the ground. The shoes also need smooth treads (that is, small ridges on the bottom) and rocker soles that enhance the natural roll of the feet while walking or jogging. They usually have a soft upper part. For walking in rough or wet terrain, it may be advisable to have deeper treads and a more robust boot to give added ankle support. Jogging and running shoes need cushioning and flexibility under the foot. They need to be light and have good grip on the sole. If you are participating in track athletic events, you may need shoes with running spikes to give added grip.

Tennis, basketball, volleyball and badminton involve a far more diverse range of movements than just running. Players need to dodge forward and backward and side-to-side. This needs shoes with flexibility and excellent support to minimize the risk of foot and leg injuries.

It is recommended that you think about the following points when buying new sports shoes:

'Jogging shoes don't give the grip you need on a muddy hockey pitch and you end up sliding all over the place. My hockey boots have bumps on the bottom to improve the grip on grass and mud.' (Esme, aged 15, hockey player)

❶ Make sure you choose the right shoe for your sporting activity.
❶ Remember that your feet are larger at the end of the day and after a workout. Buy your sports shoes when your feet are at their largest. This will ensure that, when you wear them, they won't get too tight in the middle of a match.
❶ Make sure you are wearing the variety of sock that you wear to play sport. If you try on a shoe wearing tights or thin socks, and then play sport in thick cotton socks, your shoes will be too tight.
❶ Make sure that you can wiggle all your toes comfortably within the shoe.
❶ The shoes should be comfortable immediately. You should not need to 'break them in'.
❶ Try running or a few sports moves in new shoes. They should provide the support you need and remain comfortable.
❶ Re-lacing new training shoes is a good idea. Use a criss-cross pattern to ensure even support for your foot.
❶ Make sure the shoe grips your heel firmly as you walk or run. Your heel should not slip inside the shoe.

6 Arm and wrist injuries
Building strength

Sports prone to arm, wrist and hand injuries

Diving	Weightlifting
Horse-riding	Golf
Cycling	Rugby
Rowing	American
Tennis	football
Badminton	Judo
Squash	

Injury points

Some common injuries to parts of the arm are named after certain sports, such as 'skier's thumb'. But it is not only in these particular sports that the injuries occur.

Shoulder injuries

The joint between your shoulder blade (scapula) and the top of the bone in your upper arm (humerus) is called a ball and socket joint. The top of this joint is covered by a thick layer of muscle and nerves, which run over the joint, connecting your arm to your collar bone. Your shoulder joint is very strong and can support a wide range of movements. However, some sports place a particularly heavy burden on the shoulder area. These include gymnastics (especially exercises that involve hanging and swinging from rings or bars) and power lifting. Combat sports such as wrestling, judo and kung fu can also place severe strain on the shoulder joint, as power from your shoulder muscles is used to push, pull and hold down your opponent.

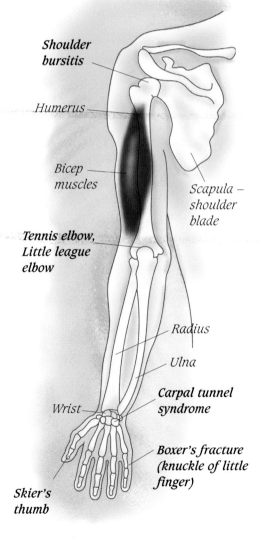

Shoulder bursitis

Humerus

Bicep muscles

Scapula – shoulder blade

Tennis elbow, Little league elbow

Radius

Ulna

Wrist

Carpal tunnel syndrome

Boxer's fracture (knuckle of little finger)

Skier's thumb

Traumatic injuries are felt as a sudden, severe pain around the shoulder area. Overuse injuries are usually felt as mild pain, which only occurs when you perform a specific movement and gradually becomes worse as you continue to use the shoulder. The commonest types of injury in the shoulder area are strains or tears of muscle fibres, tendons and ligaments. Accurate diagnosis by a doctor is essential to be sure that there is not a severe injury such as a dislocation (where the upper arm bone is pushed out of the shoulder joint) or fracture, and to identify the best way to promote recovery from the injury.

Treatment of muscle and tendon injuries often involves the RICE formula (see pages 42-43), followed by an exercise regime carefully designed to promote healing and maintain strength without aggravating the condition. Usually a series of stretching exercises are followed by a gradual programme of strengthening exercises. You should avoid sport whilst the shoulder remains painful and you should resume sporting activities gradually, in order to avoid the injury recurring.

Fine balance
In many gymnastic exercises, the arms support the whole weight of the body.

Shoulder bursitis
The shoulder has many bursae (small fluid-filled sacs that form between two moving surfaces) to ensure ease of movement between the tendons in the shoulder and the surrounding tissue. These can become inflamed through traumatic or overuse injury. This inflammation is called bursitis. Bursitis causes pain whenever you move your shoulder in a way that irritates the inflamed area. It usually takes 2–3 weeks for the condition to clear up, as long as it is rested and not irritated by movement.

'I love the parallel bar exercises, but they do place a strain on my shoulders. I do lots of strengthening and mobility exercises to make sure I stay fit and to protect my shoulder area.' (Andrea, aged 12, gymnast)

Your doctor may prescribe some anti-inflammatory medication to relieve the pain and help speed recovery. Occasionally bursitis can become an ongoing problem, in which case your doctor will refer you to an orthopaedic surgeon to see if a small operation is needed to remove the bursae.

'I think the ring exercises place the most strain on my shoulders. You have to do the exercises with such control. I have to watch my weight and fitness levels. Injuries are best avoided as you lose so much training time.' (Sven, aged 15, gymnast)

Upper arm injuries

The muscles in your upper arm – the biceps (at the front) and triceps (at the back) – are involved in pulling your arm forward from the shoulder and in bending your elbow. These muscles are particularly vulnerable in racquet sports such as tennis or badminton, gymnastics, athletic throwing events such as javelin or discus, and combat sports such as wrestling or judo.

Arm muscles are vulnerable to over-stretching, which can cause muscle strains or tears. Javelin throwers can over-stretch these muscles as they take their arm back in preparation to throw. Tennis players can over-stretch these muscles as they reach their arm back to swipe at a serve or to return a volley. Good technique and a proper warm-up are vital in order to minimize the risk of straining muscles in these situations.

An injured arm muscle can take between one and six weeks to repair properly, depending on the severity of the injury. The pain of an over-stretched muscle can be relieved by following the RICE formula (see pages 42-43). Some sports injury specialists recommend starting to stretch injured muscles soon after injury, as long as the stretching does not cause pain. Biceps can be stretched by clasping your hands behind your back with straight elbows, and very gently moving your hands away from your back. The triceps in each arm can be stretched by placing your palm as close as possible to the back of your neck, and gently pulling your bent elbow towards

Biceps stretch
Gentle exercises to stretch the muscles are an important part of recovering from injury.

your head. These exercises should be built up slowly and held for 20 seconds. The stretches should be performed slowly and in a controlled manner, as sudden stretching can cause the muscle to tighten up. They are usually performed three times a day until the injury has healed. Then you should do strengthening exercises before you resume your sport. Remember that you should always get medical advice about sporting injuries and before exercising any injured area.

Elbow injuries

Your elbow joint is a hinge joint, formed where the humerus bone of your upper arm meets the radius (outer bone) and ulna (inner bone) of your lower arm. The elbow joint is a stable joint with limited flexibility. Elbows can be injured by falling, pulling or twisting them. Sports particularly vulnerable to elbow injuries include baseball, tennis, gymnastics, rugby, wrestling and judo.

Traumatic elbow injuries are quite rare in young players, but the elbow is vulnerable to overuse injuries such as tennis or golfer's elbow and little league elbow (see page 57).

Improving my technique

'I had lots of problems with "tennis elbow" when I was a lad. I can remember thinking that it was unavoidable and that, if you wanted to play well, you had to go through some pain. I know that was wrong now, and I was probably doing myself more harm than good. When I got a professional coach, I found that my technique was wrong. When hitting a back-hand shot, my wrist would bend, but you are supposed to keep it rigid. You also need to hit the ball in the centre of the racquet and make sure you are using equipment that is the right size for you. I used to need a strap (worn over the forearm) to prevent my elbow getting sore, but as soon as I corrected my technique, the problem cleared up.' (Peter, aged 22, professional tennis player)

Wrist injuries

Your wrist is made up of eight small bones joined by ligaments, and it is extremely flexible because it has so many joints. Wrists are subject to extreme force in ball-handling games such as basketball, volleyball and netball. Archery and fencing also need good wrist strength and control. The muscles of your forearm are involved in wrist strength and mobility: they are used when you bend and twist your wrist. Sports particularly vulnerable to forearm muscle injuries include golf, rowing and tennis.

Wrist injuries are very common in young sports players, as their ability to balance is still developing and their bones are soft, so falls onto an outstretched hand can result in a wrist fracture. These are treated by aligning the affected bone and then putting a plaster cast on, to ensure that the bone heals in the correct position. Older young people (15 plus) are more likely to sprain their wrist in a similar incident.

Carpal tunnel syndrome is a common overuse injury of the wrist, particularly in racquet sports and in gymnastics. It is caused by inflammation around a nerve that runs through a channel of bone and ligament-like material (the carpal tunnel) in the centre of your wrist. It results in pain and tingling in the fingers (especially at night) and is usually treated with anti-inflammatory painkillers and by wearing a specially designed splint at night to stop the wrist from moving.

On target
You need good wrist strength to be a good archer.

Hand injuries

Your hands are complex and capable of very fine movements. They are at risk in sports that involve catching balls (especially hard balls at high speeds), such as baseball, cricket, volleyball, basketball; combat sports where they are used to grasp and push, punch or pull opponents; gymnastics; and games where you hold equipment in your hand that may be subject to force, such as hockey or lacrosse.

Young people's hands are vulnerable to fractures in a similar way to wrists. One common injury is 'boxer's fracture', which affects the knuckle of your little finger and is caused by punching. This injury actually tends to affect those engaged in combat sports rather than boxing, where contenders wear padded gloves. 'Skier's thumb' is a sprain or fracture caused by the thumb being caught on the ski pole. Occasionally this form of injury can need surgery to correct the bone alignment.

'I dislocated my finger once at judo. It hurt like hell, and I couldn't play for a few weeks, but it's fine now.'
(Kelly, aged 15)

Finger injuries are very common – particularly dislocation of the middle knuckle when struck by a ball. Dislocation is where the bones are moved out of the joint. Treatment involves a doctor repositioning the bones in the joint and then bandaging the finger to one next to it, to prevent it moving and make sure that it heals in the right position.

Sports focus: Baseball

Baseball is played between two teams of nine players. Its ancestor, rounders, is played in Britain. Baseball teams take turns to play as batters or as pitchers (throwers) and fielders. They use a very hard ball and a slim cylindrical bat.

Recovery

It can take between six and twelve weeks to recover from 'little league elbow' injury.

Throwing a baseball exerts unusual stresses on the pitcher's arm and is very difficult to do well. This means that those who pitch well are asked to do it repeatedly and this can lead to overuse injuries. One that affects younger players is 'little league elbow'. This involves injury to the growth plate on the inside of the elbow and can cause continued problems in later life. Other overuse injuries to pitchers involve shoulder injuries. These tend to be due to stress fractures or looseness in the joint and are often treated by rest and strengthening exercises.

'Baseball finger' is a traumatic injury caused by a hard ball over-extending the finger. It is also a common injury in cricket. Treatment involves splinting the finger (bandaging it so that it cannot move), rest and pain-killers. Occasionally surgery may be necessary to correct this injury. Carpal tunnel syndrome can occur as a result of pitchers repeatedly flexing their wrists. Batters occasionally get wrist fractures from repeated batting. These are treated by realignment (in hospital) and then a plaster cast is applied to ensure that the bone heals in the correct position.

Little League
Little League baseball is for players up to the age of 18. As in all sports, its rules are designed to protect players on the pitch.

To reduce or prevent baseball injuries:

❶ Always warm up and stretch properly before playing.
❶ Always use properly fitting protective equipment.
❶ Wear protective headgear with a face shield when batting, waiting to bat and running around the pitch.
❶ Build up the amount of pitching you do slowly at the beginning of a season and always stop pitching when you begin to feel tired.
❶ Limit the number of pitches per person in a game. It is a good idea to limit your pitching to 80 throws, with at least a four-day rest between games.
❶ Make sure you are wearing the appropriate catching mitt for your position.
❶ Catchers should wear a helmet, face protector, throat guard, chest protector, athletic supporter and shin guards.
❶ Wear well-fitting baseball shoes with studs for grip.
❶ Make sure the field is clear of debris that could cause slips, trips and falls.
❶ Make sure a qualified first aider is available in case of accidents.

Minimize injury, maximize enjoyment!

Sports injuries are a fact of life for professional athletes, but most can be prevented by following some basic precautions. One of the best ways to avoid injury is to focus on enjoying the game rather than on winning. Focusing only on winning can lead you to stop listening to your body, to take unnecessary risks and to push yourself too hard. All these factors make injury more likely.

Professional athletes learn to 'listen to' their body – knowing how it feels when they perform at their best, and what to look out for to prevent an injury becoming serious. You should not play when you are ill and never play through pain. It is not brave; you are just doing more damage to your body. Everyone feels aches and pains after a strenuous workout and many of these respond to the RICE formula (pages 42-43). However, sometimes injuries are more than minor. You should always tell your parents, trainer or doctor if you experience any of the symptoms listed on the right.

Reckless athletes are more likely to be injured, as are athletes who don't train enough or those who train too much. It is vital to get and follow advice from a trained coach about how much to train and when.

Despite the potential for injury, sport remains an excellent way to keep fit. When you are thinking about sports injuries, it is easy to forget that sport exists because people enjoy it. We have looked at ways to minimize the risk of sports injuries and so maximize enjoyment. Sports injuries need not be a problem. Take sensible precautions, follow the rules, use appropriate safety equipment, wear appropriate footwear, listen to your coach and have fun!

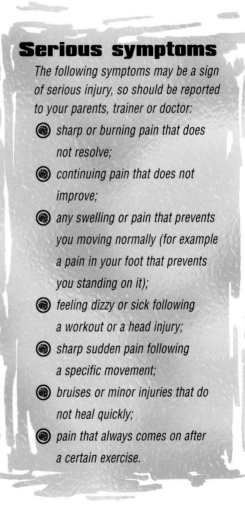

Serious symptoms

The following symptoms may be a sign of serious injury, so should be reported to your parents, trainer or doctor:

- sharp or burning pain that does not resolve;
- continuing pain that does not improve;
- any swelling or pain that prevents you moving normally (for example a pain in your foot that prevents you standing on it);
- feeling dizzy or sick following a workout or a head injury;
- sharp sudden pain following a specific movement;
- bruises or minor injuries that do not heal quickly;
- pain that always comes on after a certain exercise.

 Glossary

abdomen	the area of your body between your chest and your legs.
amenorrhoea	absence of monthly periods.
anti-inflammatory medication	medicine that relieves pain by reducing the level of inflammation around an injury.
bacteria	microscopic single-celled organisms. Some bacteria can cause diseases and infections.
blood pressure	the force exerted by blood flowing through blood vessels as it travels round your body.
bruise	sometimes called a contusion. This sometimes appears as a dark, coloured patch of skin that may be swollen and painful. It is caused by bleeding into muscle tissue.
cartilage	a tough, elastic, clear substance that has a similar function to bone but is softer and less brittle.
chronic	long-lasting and difficult to treat.
closed wound	an injury to the body that does not break the skin.
concussion	a bruise in or around brain tissue.
coordination	combining and harmonizing the movement of the whole body, in order to move without knocking into things and to perform delicate tasks.
cornea	transparent tissue that forms the front of the eye.
cramp	sudden, painful contraction of a muscle.
dislocation	displacement of a bone from its joint.

dysmenorrhoea	menstruation (periods) that are painful or involve the loss of more blood than usual.
fungi	a group of organisms that include mushrooms, toadstools and yeast. Some fungi can cause disease in humans and animals.
genitalia	the parts of our bodies that are involved in reproduction, e.g. penis, testis, vagina, uterus.
graze	an injury to the skin involving many tiny cuts to the top layers of skin.
greenstick fracture	a break in a young soft bone similar to the break that occurs in a green twig when it is twisted.
groin	the area where the thigh meets the abdomen.
growth plate	the area of each long bone that is growing in children.
gynaecological	to do with the female reproductive organs, including the vagina, uterus and ovaries.
hepatitis	an infectious disease that affects the liver.
hernia	where an internal organ (usually the intestines) protrudes through a muscle wall.
HIV	Human Immunodeficiency Virus, the virus that leads to AIDS.
joint	a structure where two or more bones meet, which allows movement.
keyhole surgery	a form of operation where the surgeon makes a very small cut (incision) to perform the operation.

laceration	a cut to the skin tissue, which may be deep.
ligament	a tough band of fibrous tissue that connects bones together.
manipulation	moving bones and joints to ensure they are in the right positions.
menstruation	monthly discharge of the lining of the womb in women (period).
mobility	ability to move.
muscle	special body tissue able to contract and relax in order to move bones.
nausea	feeling sick.
open wound	a wound that pierces through the skin, sometimes into the body tissue under the skin. This sort of wound usually causes bleeding.
ophthalmo-logist	someone qualified to treat eye and vision disorders.
orthopaedic	to do with the medical study of diseases and disorders affecting the skeleton.
osteopath	a therapist who seeks to promote healing by manipulating bones and joints to ensure that they are in correct alignment.
osteoporosis	a condition which usually affects older people, where calcium is lost from the bone. This causes the bones to become weaker and more likely to break.
overuse injuries	injuries caused by using a particular muscle or joint for too long without allowing enough time for rest and healing.

physio-therapist	a qualified therapist who uses massage, manipulation, exercise, heat, light, etc, to treat disease and promote recovery from injury.
Pilates	an exercise system started by Joseph Pilates, which uses elements of yoga, physiotherapy and Alexander posture techniques.
referred pain	pain that occurs in a different place from the problem causing it.
spasm	a sudden involuntary contraction of a muscle.
sprain	damage to a ligament caused by overstretching. It usually causes pain and swelling.
stamina	the ability to keep on doing something for a long time.
strain	similar to sprains, strains are caused by overstretching or pushing a muscle or tendon beyond its capacity.
strength	the power exerted by the body when moving or lifting something.
stroke	when the brain is damaged because a blood vessel is blocked, preventing oxygen from reaching the brain.
tendon	a bundle of fibrous tissue that attaches muscle to bone.
trauma	a wound or injury.
urinary tract	the organs involved in the production, storage and excretion of urine, including the kidneys, bladder and urethra.
warm-up	exercises performed before starting to play a sport, designed to improve performance and reduce injury.

Resources

Further reading

Robin Roberts, *Sports Injuries: Get in the Game with Robin Roberts*, Millbrook Press, 2001
An introduction to sports injuries and prevention, written by a TV presenter and aimed at getting girls to play more sport.

D. J. Boyle, *Sports Medicine for Parents and Coaches*, Georgetown University Press, 1999
A guide to preventing and treating sports injuries, by a family doctor with experience of sports medicine.

First Aid Manual The authorised manual of St John Ambulance, St Andrews Ambulance Association and the British Red Cross, 8th Edition, Dorling Kindersley, 2002
A comprehensive guide to first aid in an easy-to-use format.

Films

The Champ, 1979, directed by Franco Zeffirelli, tells the story of a boxing champion who overcomes his injuries and psychological blocks to come back for one last fight.

For the Love of the Game, 1999, directed by Sam Rani, stars Kevin Costner as a baseball player who has to fight to recover from his sporting injury to play.

Sources

The following sources were used in researching this book:

D. J. Boyle, *Sports Medicine for Parents and Coaches*, Georgetown University Press, 1999
V. Grisogono, *Sports Injuries A Self Help Guide*, John Murray Ltd, 1984
L. Patterson and P. Renstrom, *Sports Injuries Their Prevention and Treatment*, Martin Dunitz Ltd, 1983
First Aid Manual The authorised manual of St John Ambulance, St Andrews Ambulance Association and the British Red Cross, 8th Edition, Dorling Kindersley, 2002

American Academy of Orthopaedic Surgeons, 6300 North River Road, Rosemont, Illinois 60018-4262
www.aaos.org

US Department of Health and Human Services, National Centre for Health Statistics, Division of Data Services, Hyattsville MD 20782-2003
www.cdc.gov/nchs

Disclaimer
The website addresses (URLs) included in this book were valid at the time of going to press. However, because of the nature of the internet, it is possible that some addresses may have changed, or sites may have changed or closed down since publication. While the author and the publishers regret any inconvenience this may cause readers, no responsibility for any such changes can be accepted by either the author or the publishers.

Index